Alice and Pops

Tap! Tap! Tap!

Dr. Karen Campbell Kuebler

Fulton Books, Inc.
Meadville, PA

Published by Fulton Books 2021

ISBN 978-1-63710-871-0 (paperback)
ISBN 978-1-63860-471-6 (hardcover)
ISBN 978-1-63710-872-7 (digital)

Printed in the United States of America

To the Whitman family, for your innumerable contributions to the entertainment world and for nurturing generations of performers in your company and beyond.

To my mom and dad, Whit and Hazel Campbell, who nurtured and supported all my dancing dreams.

Alice Whitman—10 years old
Billy Rose Theatre Division, The New York Public
Library for the Performing Arts

Pops Whitman—4 years old

Daddy Whitman showed me
how to shuffle and flap.
So much fun to Tap! Tap! Tap!

3

I danced with my sisters in their vaudeville show.
All my costumes had a bright red bow.

Sister Bert and I tapped in the front of the stage.
While behind us, the Whitman Chorus Line was all the rage.

7

It feels so good to shim-sham shimmy with folks in their seats getting so giddy.

8

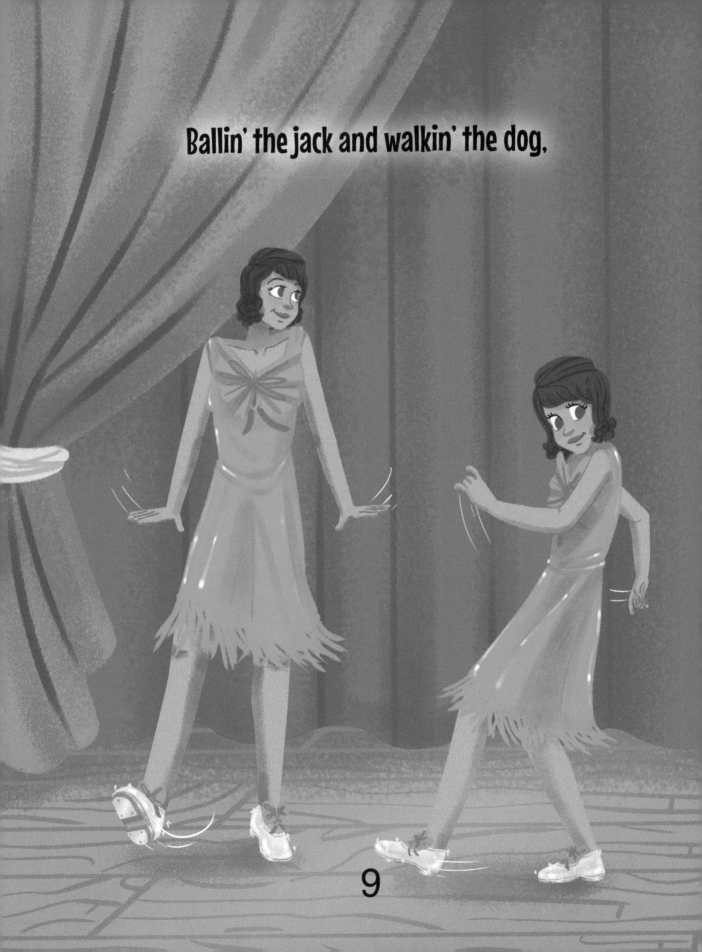

Ballin' the jack and walkin' the dog,

9

buck-and-wing, fallin' off the log.

Tap! Tap! Tap!
I beat out my solo.
Time steps too.
Oh, watch me go!

13

When my Tap! Tap! Tap!
comes to a stop,
out on the stage
spins my little boy Pops.

15

Pops dives into cartwheels, jumps, and splits
as he Tap! Tap! Taps! in a dancing blitz.

17

Buster Brown from Baltimore
sat down for the show,
saw Pops flip in the air
—no hands below!

Four-year-old Pops
glides out in his green velvet suit,
whirls his Tap! Tap! Tap!
with a smile and scoot.

19

20

21

Soaring at seventeen,
Pops and friend Louie have fun
Tap! Tap! Tap!
Dance is one plus one.

America and Europe look at the map.
Pops and Louie Tap! Tap! Tap!

Back to America
for movies and Broadway.
Amazing Tap! Tap! Tap!
night and day.

Author's Note about the Whitman Sisters Company

As young girls, Mabel, Essie, and Alberta "Bert" Whitman learned how to dance and sing from their father, Albery Allson Whitman. When they first toured, their mother, Caddie Whitman, managed the bookings and showed her daughters how to be a leader. When Mabel took over company management, she was the only female in the business. The Whitman Sisters Company was the longest-running vaudeville show on the Theatre Owners Booking Association (TOBA) circuit.

Alice Whitman (1900–1969) was the youngest sister. She joined the company at age ten and quickly became known as "The Queen of Taps." In the early 1900s, only men were allowed to do tap dance solos. Women who tap-danced were in the chorus line only. Since Alice was in her family company, she did perform solos.

Her son Albert Pops Whitman (1916–1950) joined the company at the age of three and performed show-stopping tap solos at age four. As a teenager, Pops left the family company and paired with his friend Louis Williams. They performed throughout the United States and Europe until 1950.

Tap dance vocabulary listed in order of text:

Shuffle—2 sounds, brush forward, brush back, only use the toe tap

Flap—2 sounds, brush forward, step, only use the toe tap (can be done in different directions)

Tap Dances that were made famous in the Whitman Sisters' performances:

Shim Sham Shimmy

Ballin' the Jack

Walkin' the Dog

Buck and Wing

Fallin' Off the Log

Time Steps

References

Books and newspaper articles that helped tell the story:

Afro-American. 1926. "Regent" *ProQuest Historical Newspapers: The Baltimore Afro-American*, September 4, 1926.

Afro-American. 1926. "Reviews: Royal." *ProQuest Historical Newspapers: The Baltimore Afro-American*, July 3, 1926.

Afro-American. 1927. "Whitman Sisters." *ProQuest Historical Newspapers: The Baltimore Afro-American*, November 19, 1927.

DeFrantz, T. 2002. *Dancing Many Drums: Excavations in African American dance.* Madison, WI: University of Wisconsin Press.

Frank, R. 1994. *Tap! The Greatest Tap Dance Stars and Their Stories: 1900–1955.* New York, NY: De Capo Press Inc.

George-Graves, N. 2000. *The Royalty of Negro Vaudeville: The Whitman Sisters and the Negotiation of Race, Gender, and Class in African American Theater, 1900–1940.* New York, NY: St. Martin's Press.

Pops Whitman. 1933. *The Pittsburgh Courier*, June 8, 1933.

Seibert, B. 2015. *What the Eye Hears: A History of Tap Dancing.* New York, NY: Farrar, Straus, and Giroux.

Stearns, M. and J. Stearns. 1994. *Jazz Dance: The Story of American Vernacular Dance.* New York, NY: Da Capo Press Inc.

About the Author

Karen started dancing at the age of three and never stops moving. She has always loved reading biographies and dancing stories. A passion for dance history developed in college. As a mom and teacher, Karen enjoys writing customized songs for everything you can imagine. She also loves exploring nature (especially making snow angels), traveling (especially to francophone countries), and laughing with friends. Karen lives in Baltimore, Maryland, with her husband, son, lots of books, and lots of props for story dances.

CPSIA information can be obtained
at www.ICGtesting.com
Printed in the USA
LVHW071451151021
700572LV00021B/1185

9 781637 108710